Kaddish

(Poems and Prose)

James Gerald Koch

Old Mountain Press

```
PS
3561
.0278
K33
1997
```

Published by:
Old Mountain Press, Inc.
2542 S. Edgewater Dr.
Fayetteville, NC 28303

http://www.oldmp.com

© 1997 James Gerald Koch
ISBN: 1-884778-33-X
Library of Congress Catalog Card Number: 97-75990

Kaddish.
Printed and bound in the United States of America. All rights reserved. Except for brief excerpts used in reviews, no portion of this work may be reproduced or published without expressed written permission from the author or the author's agent.

For additional copies of this book send $6.00 (includes shipping cost) to: James Gerald Koch / 16 Creekside Circle / Pittsboro, NC 27312

First Edition
Manufactured in the United States of America
1 2 3 4 5 6 7 8 9 10

Kaddish

(Poems and Prose)

INTRODUCTION

In James Koch's best poems the past, present, and future intermingle; memories slip about like shadows. Childhood, for him is not merely a convenient literary subject—it is a particular place, a reality in the mind, an embrace or a muted outcry.

His poems can be eerie and disturbing, otherworldly and mysterious; they can delight and surprise with their humor, wit and tenderness. Sometimes they are nothing less than Southern Gothic meets Headline News.

Koch tries to net the most fleeting moments—not to pin them to boards but to look at them closely in wonder and horror.

We approach his poems cautiously, at first, as we would approach an unfamiliar house at night, a house silhouetted against the sky, a house with candles burning in a single window.

I have my favorite Koch poems. Others will find favorites. He is a poet worth reading and watching as he strives to make poems wholly his own. More often than not, he succeeds.

Steven DaGamma

Trois-Rivières, Québec—Akron, Ohio
13 November 1997

Copyright © 1997 by Steven DaGama

ACKNOWLEDGMENTS

I wish to thank the following publications where some of these poems first appeared: American Literary Review, Best Poems of America, The Black Buzzard Review, Borderlands, The Dan River Anthology, The Dead Mule, Frisson, The Independent, Late knocking, Lone Wolf Review, The Old Red Kimono, The Oyster Boy Review, Poet, Poetic Realm, Savannah Literary Journal, Verve, Windhover. I wish also to thank my friend Leonardo Dicaprio for his joint effort with me in American Rimbaud. Finally, I wish to thank my mother, Joyce Koch, who was of great help in being my editor and critic in preparing this book.

CONTENTS

SEVENTEEN — YEAR OLD — POETS 9

ACROSS THE YEARS 10

POEM OF THE WOOD 11

RIMBAUD RAPED BY SOLDIERS 12

TEN YEARS LATER 13

GENIE 14

ROMAN CEMETERY 15

ALL THAT GLITTERS 16

LETTERS FROM TRAY 17

POETRY 18

METAMORPHOSIS 19

SMOKE RINGS 20

RHYMES THAT NEVER MADE MOTHER GOOSE 21

PETER'S FAREWELL 22

LAST NIGHT I DREAMED I WAS IN HEAVEN 24

ICARIAN 25

JIHAD 26

TWENTY THOUSAND LEAGUES 27

TERMINUS	28
THOUGHTS ON A LAST PHOTO OF YEATS	30
CASABLANCA	31
HUMPHREY BOGART AT THE MOUNTAINS OF MADNESS	32
MISHIMA	33
R.A.F.	34
BLOOD UPON THE SNOW	36
KADDISH	38
FIFTY YEARS AGO	39
ABDUCTION	40
MATA HARI	41
BEN	42
DUCK AND COVER	43
THE DEVIL IS A GENTLEMAN	44
PORTRAIT	45
DUTCH MASTER PAINTERS —VERMEER / SWEERTS	46
MAP AND PHOTO	48
AMERICAN RIMBAUD	50

SEVENTEEN — YEAR OLD — POETS

Rimbaud walks out on foot—
Bohemian boy with curls—
Tom Thumb in a daze—
northwards towards flanders
and the carnival of life.

He knows all the routes of September,
when the Sun, hearth of tenderness and life,
rises slowly form the inn's table
and pours out an alchemy of honeyed light
gilding the angels head.

Van Gough haystacks, parched sere-grasses,
the wheat fields waves that roll an undulate
Demeter's golden grain all the way to Picardy.
And when the wine-scented winds
waft from the vineyards,
gipsy boy dreams of degenerate lovers
with grape leaves on their brows.

Vagabond Poet,
Pan no longer piping for anyone,
and not serious about anything, at seventeen,
careless spinning such musical rhymes
as he would toss the universe in his hands.

ACROSS THE YEARS

Those summers, sundown's came late but never late
enough to find me sleepy. I would sit
in the meadows cool grass and watch
the bats wheel and dip in the wind
or walk to the dusk trees where fireflies
sprouted like berries and floated into my open hands.

When she called from the one room lit only
with the blue of the television, across whatever
distance there was, I was never ready
though my legs were heavy from play, my hands dusty
with the dozen of fluttering bodies I had held,
pulsing like the veins in my own thin wrists.

Sleep, she said, though sometimes later the wind
rose and touched me in my sheets. *Sleep,* though
sometimes the curtains wheezed and the trees whispered
through the summer night. When I woke, I found
the world shiny with the pools of my dreams.
That was the time of sun and rain, of play and sleep.

Tonight the rain is falling gently in the dark, as if
through the wind and dim of my past. The windows
are still opened and the edges of the curtains
in my room are damp and hanging heavy.
Whose voices do I hear, calling across the years?

I will not sleep again tonight. I want to find
that child and be him again. I want to get up and go
back beneath the trees, and walk there until the morning.
I want to come to that land and open the door,
and find myself a man who crossed the years.

POEM OF THE WOOD

When, days later, we reached the end of the path
and lay at last among voluptuous leaves,
we swore we never should see days go by so fast again.
By day our words were marked by time, but all night long
the language that we spoke was, like the brightest star,
fixed, it seems, forever, in one place.
Did you find out alone the high road back?
I know you sleep somewhere among a thousand cities now,
while I lie here, still, tangled in these leaves.

RIMBAUD RAPED BY SOLDIERS

The gods listen to man and to the infinite world!
                                            -Rimbaud-

Rimbaud raped by soldiers
at the age of sixteen,
pity is a place
the Gods have never seen.

Bacchus a drunken God
is belching while he raves,
lisens not to Rimbaud's
abracadabratic waves.

Wise old Zeus absent too,
present only in books,
page by yellow page fades
to dust in quiet nooks.

Pity dissolves in spit:
heaven closed its door,
under jeering soldiers
Rimbaud bleeds on the floor.

Rimbaud raped by soldiers
at the age of sixteen,
pity is a place
the Gods have never seen.

TEN YEARS LATER

The sun is falling in the west tonight
like Lucifer, lightning struck, whirling down
with wings blazing the flames of Turner's boats.

It's middle November, all's tinged with fig
color or bruised brown, except the bare trees
rattling in the wind like moss-covered bones.

Adam limps by on blistered heels, and tries
to forget the strain rutabagas make
on his back; flint bits bite his soles like snakes.

Cold air hits his face, near gnarled oaks;
he sniffs leaves heaped at his feet, and recalls
trimming, with Eve, the lush hedges that looked

always ripening—but now no light spills
through the woods, it's gone, expunging past
pleasure so all that remains are the peels

of what is gone, the thorns of quarrels, lost
promises. Now dark, what lies ahead hurts
him: Eve gray, worn; limp with thick waist.

Yet, eyes closed, he knows still that the desire
her flesh will kindle, just as long ago,
when the moon sets, shadows lengthen, and stars

  appear in the sky like seed from Cain's small hand.

GENIE

A winter's sky looms
a canvas in a shadowed loft,
weary clouds seek rest
on red vapor mountains
stained pink and purple
by the bleeding sun.
Black bones dance
on the limbs of a towering oak
shedding its last leaf,
reluctantly.
In the distance
pillows drift across a childs bed,
and the red center calls
for a moment's reflection
before the frail shards of color
yield to the consuming night.

ROMAN CEMETERY

It is dusk
and the wind
rips across
the chest
of the stone boy.

Each year, the ivy thickens,
its vines pulling more tightly
against him.
The alter, once covered
with lamb and wine
crumbles.

I look at his face.
I think I know him,
though his body
is tired and weak
from waiting in the wind.

He'd like to sit
to heave his shoulders foreword.
The wind sighs through his lips.
I want to kiss them,
across ten centuries
one last long good-bye.
I want to link my arm through his.
He has become too frail.

ALL THAT GLITTERS

Our teacher opened jars of colored glitter
and each of us took out one or more blown out eggs.
I longed to make an ornament so brilliant,
my parents would hang it on our Christmas tree
just above the golden bird made by my sisters
artistic hand.
First I started with some gleaming sequins, then
added tiny rocaille beads. I worked with concentration,
gluing tinsel to hang like icicles, adding plastic pearls.
But when I glanced at all the other kids I saw something
strange began to happen—these ornaments did not resemble
the ones our parents unpacked each year from boxes.
Silver glitter mixed in glue turned gray; ribbons gleamed
on foil, but the foil tore under frustrated fingers.
My friend beside me, who had finished drawing a
lopsided tree with globs of glue, was now dusting glitter
along the lines, perfecting a mistake.
I looked at my Charlie Brown ornament.
The hanger was askew, and glitter flaked away like salt
leaving only scabs of glue. The sequins made a ugly
glob at the top and the tinsel streamer looked like dirty string.
I held it up, shocked with what my hands had wrought.
My hands had betrayed me and turned my vision to
utter mockery. At home my parents made it worse
by praising my ugly work. They hung it on the tree
beside the beautiful bird. But every time I passed the
 tree I shuddered and finally moved the gaudy, trashy
thing to a inner bough deep in the tree.
Afterwards, I rested on the rug, near the fire, looking
at the beautiful blinking lights until I yawned and
dozed and finally dreamed of the ornament I'd meant
to make, hanging high on the tallest tree in a
silent forest.

LETTERS FROM TRAY

Blue sea, no surf, shells
for sale at the southernmost point
full of deep pink roaring:

his letters arrive now monthly
telling me of his days and nights
where Hemingway's cats still roam.

*The spiders here hang lazily
he writes. The guys I meet
drink heavily in midnight bars*

as music stains the streets. His metaphors
come forced and hard, his reach
for rhythm stumbles; but underneath

each flowing word I feel
the radiant smile he left me
as winter now ices the trees.

To visit him? Eat conch chowder
and drink spiced rum as palms
creak in the breeze? He doesn't

ask, suggests he's happy, lets
me know he doesn't sleep alone
in the room with a gingerbread porch.

Far away in my own mornings
as black night give way to gray
I read his words, drink day-old

coffee, tell myself that pelicans
are clumsy birds, red hibiscus
wearies eye and heart with lurid bloom.

POETRY

A morning like this,
the phone ringing at six-thirty,

with moderately good news
—just as the rain lets up—

meaning an hour of peace,
a sweet fragrance coming in the window

on the warm breeze drifting
over us in the tangled bed-clothes,

a Cardinal singing outside,
something by Sibelius on the radio,

and you saying you feel "frisky,"
a single morning like this

could make some poetry.

METAMORPHOSIS

Glorious April, pierced
with daffodils.
The apple has not bloomed yet
but its pulse is felt.

Three girls in summer clothes run,
as if to catch the sun.
Their laughter wafts through a field
with a green willow. Liquid shades
of hair bob behind them.

One has found a cocoon.
They study it with interest.
They consider putting it in a jar
but decide to leave it on the tree.

They climb the willow,
find it smooth enough
for gymnastics. They challenge
each other in Olympic-like stunts.

Tomorrow, Easter.
They will emerge from their houses
in other clothes — light flowery
dresses, long enough to hide skinned knees.
The cocoon will have opened.

Womanly they sit in church,
learn of another tree,
resurrection, another love—
sweet and glorious as April's blood.

SMOKE RINGS

I like to watch the intimacy
of couples who smoke: how deftly he gets
the lighter from her purse as she
explores his pockets for cigarettes.

They do this casual loving while
they entertain or mind the kids.
It has its own peculiar style,
the promise shared without the words.

What if they share each other's ailments—
the health in style is hardly shared.
I love these non-aerobic dancers,
smoke rings rising till joining and paired.

RHYMES THAT NEVER MADE MOTHER GOOSE

Little Miss Muffet sat on her tuffet,
her panties all tattered and torn,
it wasn't a spider who sat down beside her,
but little boy blue with his horn.

PETER'S FAREWELL

Dear Wendy, I really have enjoyed our little island,
the flamingos in the bay and tigers in the trees,
the moon, trapped in a net of stars,
high above our fire-circle;

and being the father of the boys,
and you the mother, of them and me...
sewing our wooden buttons on
and tucking us in our bedrolls.

These things I shall remember
at the government orphan school,
when I lie still on my narrow cot
and in the chilly night hear

not the waves that splash this beach,
but the crying sound, muffled
beneath blankets, and swift hands
coaxing pleasure from flesh.

Dear Wendy, I have seen what we must become,
not to confide in faithful fairies
or try to fight all captain Hooks
with swords and alligator allies.

All my life I haven't listened;
I have not heard time.
Now, louder than a clock's ticking,
it slides on faster than the alligator crawls.

I'm sad, you know to leave you here,
but you'll survive, sweeping, cooking
little meals of dew and mushrooms;
a new boy will out punch all the other
boys to win my place as father
across from you at the table.

You are almost a woman Wendy,
so playing their mother
may be enough for you always;
but if some night, waking
to hear the snoring by your hut,
you find your feet are restless,

then you leave too. look me up;
came to tea, laugh at the stiffness
of my neck inside my collar.
I'll lose my heart to your dapper dress
and the dignified way you smile,
pouring tea into my cup.

But do not wait too long to follow me,
or you may come, with your long hair
and blushing laughter, to a self-made-man
with whiskers and a watch chain
who's forgot the green and magic island
and lost the heart of a child.

LAST NIGHT I DREAMED I WAS IN HEAVEN

I sit next to Yeats in Monet's garden. We are
listening to Oscar Wilde telling some story, Proust sits
smiling dipping madeleines in tea. Dylan Thomas goes
To the house for a beer whispering over his shoulder
"now wait for me Willie before you read Lastpis Lapis"
Out by the field, Rimbaud and Verlaine horseplay testing
their new legs. Wilfred Owen and Rupert Brooke throw
a baseball back and forth and then to some boy.

Mark Twain smokes a big cigar as he judges Monet's
and Van Gogh's canvases in the Sun. Van Gogh jabs
Monet and teases "oh Claude, I think I've got you today".
The band is warming up; Shubert, Wagner, Elgar,
and Bach. Strauss waltzes in leading the last five
hundred years of Vienna boys choir giggling.
In a corner around the house, Shakespeare talks with
Orson Wells about how he intends to play Hamlet tonight.

At dusk Julia Child brings out platters of sweet breads a la
Napolitane, salad Livoniere and a tureen of Gaspacho of Malaga.
Then, from the field a twelve year old Jesus comes radiant,
smiling, sweaty from playing baseball and sits down beside me.
He takes off his cap and reaches into his pocket and
hands me a piece of grape bubble gum. Dumbfounded,
I take it and he ask me if I am happy.
His smile and laugher is the best part of the dream.

ICARIAN

Boys will climb trees, even if
they are forbidden. How can we watch
them closely enough ? In an eye's

blink they are lost, high in the emerald
darkness. The thin boughs, the leaves
are as solid as their own jumbled beds

as safe a place to dream. They gaze
at a green sky through canopies lit
from heaven. They offer their own small

hands to the light, watch the green
thread their fingers, hear the pulse grow
in their temples.

Useless to call — higher and higher — they will not
come down. We do not like to imagine
their sun-lit hair, their wild eyes

watching us. We will look for them
on the ground. We can recognize
a leg bent under a body, a cry of pain.

JIHAD

I carry a suitcase through the
busy streets, past the checkpoint
into the open, leafy avenue.
I walk into a outdoor cafe
packed nicely with a noon-day crowd.
I find a seat at a table
across from a child whose
watercolors and papers are scattered
on the ground.
He paints rapidly then holds it up
to show me as his parents talk.
I push my chair back to leave as
the child begins another piece.
I slip out easily past the crowded
tables and chairs, leaving the suitcase
behind.
My pace quickens to match my heart
and I am once again moving through
the streets as primary colors rise
behind me.
It is all the colors
that child could ever paint.

TWENTY THOUSAND LEAGUES

The most marvelous moment
must have been entering the great iron fish
for the first time,
the overwhelming of the senses,
blundering into an unknown
beautiful and intricate as a shell,
understanding you had
underestimated the possibilities
all along.

After the long search,
convinced all the time it was known,
to find it was created,
to leave that steel deck
and enter that world below.
Dark at first, your eyes
must gradually have taken it all in,
brass meters glowing phosphorescent green,
a quiet humming in the background,
the beating of another heart,
Nemo's weird organ distantly playing.
Suddenly, the machine must have lurched foreword,
thrust unknowing towards Atlantis
and its already broken dreams.

TERMINUS

Adam follows his voice into the dark.
After the final sound
he hears the alphabet of exhaustion.

>The Milky Way revolves
>once every 500 million years
>maybe eight or nine times
>since creation.

There is the slipping
into ambiguity
as the distance swells.

>Thirty thousand light years
>from Earth
>to the center of the galaxy.

The soft blur in the corner
suddenly demands attention.

>The nearest star
>Alpha Centauri
>26 trillion miles.

Caught behind his eyelid
the afterimage
that won't clarify.

>"Andromeda, where is Perseus?"
>the one who is to carry us away
>from this cooling stone.
>we ride the edge
>of this spiral galaxy
>as it plays its
>Akashic record,

He can't hear her
drifting so far away,
diamond compression.

      A sun implodes
      becomes a white dwarf
      One handful weighs 25 tons.
      Finally he give up lifting.

Tonight geese grab
at the quick sketch of stars.
Over the slow tilt of Earth
they fall toward Polaris
fade into their voices.

THOUGHTS ON A LAST PHOTO OF YEATS

The photograph is fading now, its cracked
across a corner near his wild white head.
In spite of autumn heat, his coat is closed
completely — like his eyes — as if the act
of sitting in the sun were strange. Instead,
he may have slipped away from lunch to doze
in what he hoped was privacy, this guest
whose verse had sung the fierce heroic stands
of fabled warlords on his wind-raw isle.
It's difficult to gasp that mind at rest,
at last, from politics in which the hand
of each was raised against his brother, while
he craved some queenly woman for his bed
yet roamed alone the Celtic spirit-lands.

CASABLANCA

In the movie Casablanca, Ilsa and Rick
will always have Paris, always. Bogart-Blaine
may drink his bourbon straight and feel no pain,
but in the final reel (his neatest trick)
he'll always set young Ilsa free: he'll pick
the hero's life and put her on the plane.
Let the years roll by, his image will remain:
Rick Blaine is free from times arithmetic.

Indeed, with film one seems to watch the man
grown young as one grows old. Through the highest art
has always sought this dream of timelessness,
Should it not pity the aging movie fan?
As times goes by, the scenes he knows by heart
will mock lost youth, when a kiss was still a kiss.

HUMPHREY BOGART AT THE MOUNTAINS OF MADNESS*

And yet, he does not shiver in
his lightweight suit, thin city shoes.

Penguins, drawn by the glow of his
cigarette after cigarette

cluster about him. Thousands. When
one begins to applaud, at first

shyly, then ferociously, they
all join in, flapping and slapping

their flippers on the frozen floor.
And when Bogart casually

offers his worn fedora in
tribute to the giant albino penguin

the augmented claps are matched by
cries of "Bogie! Bogie! Bogie!

until the ice tunnels echo.

*Hollywood almost made a film based on H.P. Lovecraft's bizarre south pole horror story"At The Mountains of Madness". The film was never made but before the idea was canceled Bogart was being considered for a lead in the film.

BLOOD UPON THE SNOW*

He couldn't have been more than twelve
but he slid under tank bellies, nicely,
like it was a game. After those magnetic
mines did their work, he and the other
peached faced orphans would pretend to laugh and
not to shake. He stood straight and still
in line to receive his tank destroyer badge,
just like any soldier would.
After the last tank was through with him
and not being fully grown anyway,
there wasn't much left to bury.
Stalin, you couldn't ask for better soldiers.

* Due to Stalin's purges and the German attack
on Russian during W.W.2 many orphans joined the army
just to survive. A special unit of such orphans were
used as tank killers during the war. Few survived.

KADDISH

Your open hands raised in the air
like two white doves
frame your meager face,
your face contorted with fear,
grown old with knowledge beyond your years.
How old? eight? nine? ten?
Not yet compelled to wear
the star that will seal
your fate.

No need to brand the very young.
They will always follow their mothers.

You are standing apart
against the flock of women and their brood
with blank, resigned stares.
You know. You know your fate,
It's written on your face.
In your dark eyes — a vision of Sheol.
You have seen Death already.

FIFTY YEARS AGO

That disc of silver
that skipped and hopped
across the fleecy sky
was not a bird, was not a plane,
or sun-spots before his eyes.
At mach 1 he caught it there
as he clutched the throttle between his crotch
and watched it circle him once, than twice,
before it stopped to play hopscotch.
He landed quick
and wrote his report out,
to only sit in a bar in silence
and rotate slowly a glass of gin.
But sleepless nights
on a too small bed
told the flyboy
he would not mock again—
the spirit of the age
had found a place to land.

ABDUCTION

Be thankful, Unicorn,
that you do not exist.

Chimera, Cyclops, Gnome,
your terrors live in dreams.
Whatever ancient minds conceived
we move to darker themes.

Be grateful, Basilisk,
that you were never born.

Behemoth, Dragon, Sphinx,
be happy you're ideal;
these times engender forms
more terrible, more real.

MATA HARI

In the morning, the mid-October sun touched
its flame to the steeple-tops, the courtyard
cobblestones beneath the prison wall rouged

themselves once more, stained by the blood of dawn.
Mata Hari, fallen to her knees only an hour ago—
thought her cry awakened even the silent dead.

Yet, all the townsfolk of Vincennes slept on
in that pre-dawn charade, as a sleepy squad
of soldiers rubbed their eyes to focus, to

see before them a woman of middle-age,
still beautiful — her watery, pearl — colored
blouse billowing below her rueful smile, soft nod.

They took aim upon the commander's shout,
while she let her mind go wandering back,
free from the grip of rope, to her childhood:

Leeuwarden and her uncle's windmill where
she hid her cigars, scooched down into
the gold hay; and later Amsterdam, city

of music, carriages, paintings, prayer;
and Java where she danced the night beneath
a volcano, her silk Sarong unwinding: flash

of the tiger, the rare green peacock: Paris
moonstruck with lilies; and Berlin. Above,
she heard the shots. She regretted nothing.

BEN*

See how he loves me.
Sunlight racing
down the front porch steps,
he flies into my arms
engulfing me like summer.
In his small boys eyes — joy —
a joy that we share.
His head nest on my shoulder,
dusksoft,
darkening my vision.
I would die for him.
He hangs on tight
as if I might.

*age 10

DUCK AND COVER

"Eb, Eb, Eb, dats all folks!"
              -Porky Pig-

In seventh grade Sister blasted her whistle
and our entire class dove madly
under our tiny desks. Our hands made
frail prayer clasped helmets to cut
the risk of blast damage.
We raised our bottums toward a wall of windows.
Heaven seemed to approve — The sun was warm.
We closed our eyes. The flash
and blast would only
singe our butts funny
like when Porky sat on fire
and jumped to heaven in wild pain
right up through angel filled clouds.

Our foreheads and crucifixes
touched the floor
in blind supplication—
most important to keep
absolutely quiet and still!
Sister would whisper
that should such a moment come
we ought also to pray.

Our little bottoms fibrillated
as if stabbed by old Nick.
Sister must have studied
that trembling-but she never
explained to us boys
how our precious jewels
hung like sweet offerings
before the atomic God.

THE DEVIL IS A GENTLEMAN
(Marquis De Sade 1740-1814)

His hands were feminine, he moved with grace,
danced the gavotte, could turn a villanelle.
Blood smeared his powered hair, his ruffled lace.

Pity the woman lured to his embrace —
he'd whip her moan of lust into pains red yell.
His hands were feminine, he moved with grace

while scenting flesh to injure and debase.
What Freud would scry long after, Sade knew well.
Blood smeared his powered hair, his ruffled lace

Reading *Justine* or *Juliette*, I grimace
at thoughts that give off such a sulfurous smell.
His hands were feminine, he moved with grace.

He blew up God and the whole human race
in books that erupted from is Bastille cell.
Blood smeared his powdered hair, his ruffled lace.

I've read him, cold sweat running down my face.
He lights our dark half, this gentleman from hell.
His hands were feminine, he moved with grace.
Blood smeared his powdered hair, his ruffled lace.

PORTRAIT

When Vincent Van Gogh was twenty nine
he had a woman for a while.
She was a prostitute, and she smoked
cigars, and she was pregnant,
but he gave her a place to stay, and
he gave her food, and as much money
as he could spare, and he took her
to the hospital when she was sick.
In turn, she posed for him.

In one drawing
he has her seated naked on a rock
or tree stump or something.
She sits with her knees up,
her head down, buried in her arms.
Her hair hangs loose,
in twisted ropes down her back,
her useless breasts sag.
Her buttock are poor, her belly
large, her feet are painful to see.

She looks as if she had been standing
in one spot all day long,
watching the most tortured man alive
smoke, and paint, smoke
and paint.
It's a classic pose, for practice.
Vincent called it "Sorrow."

DUTCH MASTER
PAINTERS—VERMEER/SWEERTS

The piety of small joys.
Lace. Bread and milk.
Lined faces bowed in prayer—
a young nobleman
with visions of the world.
A portrait of a boy.

No more than this
ever. All day
by a window
a woman weighing pearls.
God's equation
of peace and light.

MAP AND PHOTO

A trench-map from the Battle of the Somme
(It doesn't matter where I found it)
has a dead fly still stuck
at the bottum left-hand corner
by a place called Longueual,
dark from red blood sucked
out of British soldiers long since gone
over the top or to Tipperary—
where many went to
in those distant days.

Photograph.
Whoever he was
sat on an upturned tin
and smoked a pipe.
Spring months were finished beyond the parapet
and winter not yet willing to let him through
the mist of that valley he would try to cross—
while the earth shook from bites of artillery
as if to shrug all men forever off its back.

He spread the map across his muddy knees
and a bloated corpse-fed fly dropped there
as if its feet were made of fur or soot,
and crawled over villages he hoped to see
easier than half a million men did.

With bemused eyes he followed it
in a moment of mercy and apprehension as if
to divine by which point it would stop
and finally take off from—
what possible place it would be
where the end might come on him.

His hand refused to follow up these thoughts,

the messenger was smashed upon his map—
now pinned on my peaceful study wall
after eighty years gone by,

When night came he lit one of the lanterns
by which to count his men into the trench,
and crouching on the last day of June
in the deep earth slit that stank
of soil and Woodbines, cordite and bitter shit,
he held the green wick close to his exhausted face
which mirrored the failing marrow of his life—
then shut the light into the safety of its case,
and ceased to think.

AMERICAN RIMBAUD

Such a boy he is in summer:
at dawn the sunflowers open in his voice
and he sings the sun's bright ribbons up.
All through the radiant wind-crisp day,
rivers cut sandy channels in his hands,
grain fields burgeon in his hair,
thunderstorms bristle in his stride
to the top of sunset golden hills
where he sits until night hangs
it's black banners out.
Under the spangled prairie sky
coyotes hunt in his dreams
and whippoorwills whittle his heart.

Under winters star-chilled vault he
haunts the shadowed farmyard
and fumbles at the barndoor latch
where cattle steam and shuffle in their stalls.
He cups his face in his hand and writes
by the single lamp, till with a
flint-edge cry slams his diary shut.
Under the moons gaunt shell
he wanders off toward icy lights
(a nearby prairie town scatters up the sky)
he will rasp and whisper along its streets,
looking for something, someone,
to take him in.

James Gerald Koch was born December 7, 1964 in Roanoke Virginia. He holds bachelors degrees in Psychology, Criminal Justice, and Military Science, and a Masters in Political Science from Appalachian State University. From 1990-1991 he saw action in the Gulf War as a company commander with the 24th mechanized division.

His poetry has appeared in local, national, and international poetry journals. His primary works to date include:
In Grecian Glory (Poetry) 1994
Toward The Origins of The Golden Dawn (History) 1994
The Homecoming (Poetry) 1995
Rimbaud (Poetry) 1996
Kaddish (Poetry) 1997
He also worked with Mary Greer to produce Magical Women of The Golden Dawn (History) 1995.
Beyond his literary interest he pursues running, pipe collecting, and studying the life and works of Arthur Rimbaud.
He resides in Pittsboro, North Carolina and is a member of the North Carolina Writers Network.